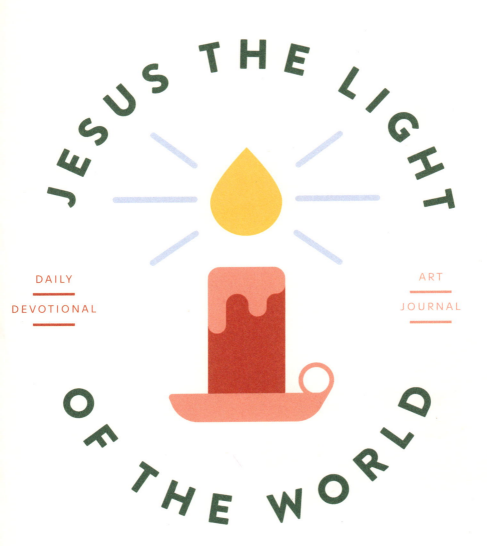

©First15 2023

Illustrations by Jennie Miller
Typesetting and design by Amanda Barnhart

No part of this publication may be reproduced, distributed, or transmitted in any form or by any means, including photocopying or electronic or mechanical method without prior written permission of the editor; except in the case of brief quotations embodied in critical reviews and certain other noncommercial uses permitted by copyright law. For permission requests, please write to us.

Unless otherwise stated, Scripture quotations are taken from the International Children's Bible®. Copyright © 1986, 1988, 1999 by Thomas Nelson. Used by permission. All rights reserved.

THE HOLY BIBLE, NEW INTERNATIONAL VERSION®, NIV® Copyright © 1973, 1978, 1984, 2011 by Biblica, Inc.® Used by permission. All rights reserved worldwide.

Jesus, the Light of the World

DAILY DEVOTIONAL + ART JOURNAL

Charity Rios

first15

Let's spend time with God!

This journal belongs to

Name

Year **Age**

Table of Contents

8 Introduction

10 How to Use This Devotional

14 Day 1: The Light Who Is Always with You

18 Day 2: The Light Who Shines through You

22 Day 3: The Light Who Was Sent because God Loves You

26 Day 4: The Light Who Has Good Gifts for You

30 Day 5: The Light Who Will Do Big Things through You

34 Day 6: The Light Who Brings You Peace

38 Day 7: The Light Who Provides

42 Day 8: The Light Who Is a Good Shepherd

46 Day 9: The Light Who Is Worthy of Worship

50 Day 10: The Light Who Is Good News

54 Day 11: The Light Who Came as a Servant King

58 Day 12: The Light Who Gives You the Gift of Faith

62 Day 13: The Light Who Is Trustworthy

66 Day 14: The Light Who Gives You Family

70 Day 15: The Light Who Is Worthy of Your Time

76 Day 16: The Light Who Speaks to You

80 Day 17: The Light Who Delights in You

84 Day 18: The Light Who Is Worthy of Your Best Gifts

90 Day 19: The Light Who Leads You

94 Day 20: The Light Who Is Your Wonderful Counselor

98 Day 21: The Light Who Is Full of Power

102 Day 22: The Light Who Is the Way

106 Day 23: The Light Who Is the Prince of Peace

110 Day 24: The Light Whose Kingdom Will Grow

114 Day 25: The Light Who Gives Eternal Life

Introduction

Hey, Kids and Parents!

I am thrilled that you are here. (I wish you could join me in a happy dance!)

Have you ever had a flashlight, glow stick, or glow-in-the-dark toy? My kids love glow-in-the-dark monster trucks. They beg me to close their doors and turn off all the lights so their toys' lights shine bright.

Light shines brightest in the darkness.

Jesus was born about two thousand years ago. It was a dark time for God's people and not just because they didn't have electricity yet. It was a dark and sad time in their hearts and country. The people in charge, the Romans, didn't like God's people and made life hard for them. But they knew from the promises that God had made to their great-great-

great-great (probably more *greats* than this)-grandmas and -grandpas that God would send a Savior to rescue them from the sin in their hearts and from the enemies that made life terrible.

Maybe you've heard that the season of Advent is a time for getting ready to celebrate the birth of Jesus, the promised Savior, on Christmas Day. His birth is important because he was the light that came to the darkness and brought salvation, hope, peace, joy, and love to a hurting world.

Although the birth of Jesus was the most important birth in the history of the world, in this devotional, you will learn how God used ordinary people and places to be important parts of the birth of Jesus. I hope you'll see that the gift of Jesus is for everyone. He loves you and has incredible plans for your life right now, even as a kid!

There are many wonderful ways to celebrate Advent. This devotional will focus on seeing and understanding how Jesus was the light that came to a hurting and broken world. We'll have fun and also stretch our minds and hearts to learn more about the many ways that Jesus shines his light.

My prayer for each of you is that you end this Advent devotional with an excitement to celebrate Jesus and worship him this Christmas season.

I am praying for you!

Joyfully,

Charity Rios and the First15 Team

Hello!

Welcome to *Jesus, the Light of the World,* a twenty-five-day devotional + art journal written just for you! This might be your first devotional ever, or maybe it's your tenth. Either way, we pray you will grow in your love for God and his word each day!

Spending time with God every day through reading, praying, and practicing our faith is so important for us to draw close to him and know him more. So, every day for the next twenty-five days, you'll do just that.

Each day has the following elements to help you make the most of your time with God this Christmas season:

1 **Devotional:** Read a scripture for the day and a short devotional that will teach you about God, yourself, and the Bible.

2 **Prayer:** Spend time talking and listening to God.

3 **Go:** Enjoy a fun activity to help you apply the truth you've learned.

Read. Pray. Go. Repeat!

As you think about the next twenty-five days you will spend with God, what excites you the most?

Draw or write what makes you excited.

At the end of this devotional, our prayer is that you will be excited to keep spending time with God every day. God bless you as you read, pray, and go each day with a God who loves you so much!

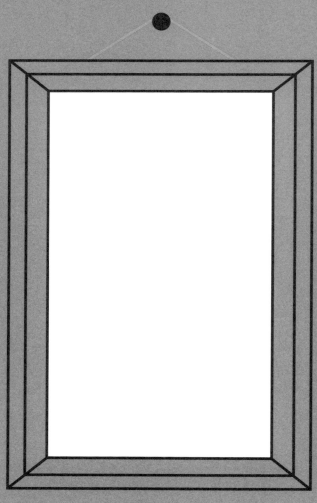

✏️ **Draw** a picture of yourself with your new journal.

The true Light was coming into the world. **The true Light gives light to all.**

—John 1:9

Day 1: The Light Who Is Always with You

SCRIPTURE

"But the Lord himself will give you a sign: The virgin will be pregnant. She will have a son, and she will name him Immanuel."

—Isaiah 7:14

Is there a gift you are hoping to receive this Christmas? *Write inside this present what gift you are most hoping to find under the tree.*

The Bible verse you read today tells us about a very special gift that was promised by a prophet named Isaiah. Look at the Bible verse again—what do you think the special gift was?

Check the answer:

- A baby
- A kangaroo
- A remote control car
- A bike

If you checked "baby," you are correct. The name of this baby gives us a clue about why he was so special. One of his names is Immanuel. Immanuel means "God with us."

Write the meaning of Immanuel:

The gift of baby Jesus is the greatest gift we could ever receive. The reason Jesus is the greatest gift is because through his birth, death, and resurrection we can always have God with us. This is why one of Jesus's names means "God with us."

How does it make you feel knowing that Jesus is with you all day today and every day?

Circle every face that shows how you feel:

Happy

Peaceful

Safe

Thankful

Let's pray together!

God, thank you so much that you sent Jesus your son to be Immanuel, God with me. Thank you for wanting to be a part of my life every day. Help me remember that you are with me always.

In Jesus's name, amen.

GO

Draw a picture of Jesus being with you today as you play, go to school, or spend time at home.

Day 2: The Light Who Shines through You

SCRIPTURE

The true Light was coming into the world. The true Light gives light to all.

—John 1:9

Have you put up any Christmas lights yet? Maybe on your tree, your house, or mantel? One of our family's favorite things to do at Christmas is to drive around our city and find the lights on neighbors' houses.

Is it easy or hard to spot houses that have Christmas lights?

Check the answer:

◯ EASY-PEASY!   ◯ HARD! I need a telescope.

It's easy-peasy, lemon-squeezy, right? Seeing which houses have lights on them is easy because it's so dark in December. It's the same way with Jesus in us! The light of Jesus fills our lives, and we can be a light to a world that often feels dark because of sin and sadness.

Bringing the light of Jesus to the world may mean praying for a friend who's sad or sick. Or being a light can look like serving others by giving clothes, toys, or food to someone in need. Sharing the light of Jesus can happen on the playground, at home, or even on the basketball court by speaking words of encouragement to classmates, family, or teammates, or inviting the new kid to play with you.

Let's pray together!

Jesus, fill me with your light today so that I can shine your love, joy, and peace to the people I see today.

In Jesus's name, amen.

GO

Our friends have a tangled mess of lights. Help them untangle their lights and get them to the correct house.

Now think about one person you can share the light of Jesus with today. It could be a sibling, your parents, classmates, or teammates.

Write the name of that person or draw their picture in the house.

Day 3: The Light Who Was Sent because God Loves You

SCRIPTURE

But some people did accept him. They believed in him. To them he gave the right to become children of God.

—John 1:12

DEVOTIONAL

Does it usually snow at your house around Christmas? Snow is beautiful and special because each snowflake is different and unique. No two snowflakes are alike! Think of your friends and family—are any of them the same? Even twins may look identical, but their hearts, personalities, and thoughts are different.

Look for the differences in these two pictures. *Circle all the differences you see!*

Every person has been uniquely made by God. *Unique* means the special and good ways God has made you that are different from anyone else. You are so loved by God that he sent his son Jesus for you. Jesus lived on earth and showed people the love of God. He showed this by healing sick people, by loving every person—even people that most people didn't like—and by serving everyone. He also overcame the biggest obstacle of all: death itself when he died and rose from the dead for you. When we accept Jesus's perfect gift of salvation, we become children of God.

Let's pray together!

Father God, thank you for making me in your image. Thank you for the unique and perfect way you created me as your child. Help me to understand how you made me.

In Jesus's name, amen.

GO

Think about the unique way that God made you. He gave you special gifts and talents. He knows everything about you and can tell you how you were created and made and why he made you that way.

This could be how he made you look, the talents he gave you (do you like to draw, play a sport, dance, sing, build Lego structures, or play a musical instrument?), or the personality that makes you unique (maybe you're quiet and think a lot; maybe you love telling jokes and making people laugh; maybe you're good at leading things or always have great ideas). If you're not sure, ask one of your parents or siblings what is special about you.

On the points of the snowflakes, **write down the unique ways God has made you.**

After writing on the snowflake, consider making a snowflake as a gift for a friend or family member. **Write on the snowflake:** "God made you special. You are special because _____."

25

Day 4: The Light Who Has Good Gifts for You

SCRIPTURE

The Word became a man and lived among us. We saw his glory—the glory that belongs to the only Son of the Father. The Word was full of grace and truth.

—John 1:14

DEVOTIONAL

Where do you spend Christmas? Sometimes at Christmastime, we travel to see family or friends that we may not get to see very often. If you're going to travel this Christmas, how are you going to get there?

Color which one you will use:

Is there a person you're excited to see and celebrate Christmas with?

Write their name here:

As excited as we may be to see family and friends at Christmas, the people alive when Jesus was born were eagerly waiting for him to come. They had waited around

27

DEVOTIONAL

five thousand years for Jesus to be born. Wow! That is a long time. However, they didn't expect him to come as a baby, so some people didn't believe it was even him.

For the people who believed Jesus was the Son of God, who came to earth to save them from their sin, they were very excited! Two of those people were a woman named Anna and a man named Simeon. They had been waiting and praying for Jesus to come their entire lives. As you can guess, they were very excited when they met Jesus!

Let's pray together!

Jesus, give me the same excitement to talk to you and be with you that Anna and Simeon had when they met you for the first time. Thank you that I have the chance to talk to you and be with you every day.

In Jesus's name, amen.

GO

Often, we will bring special gifts to our family and friends at Christmastime.

Because of Jesus's birth, we have access to amazing gifts that he fills us with! Even though Christmas is a celebration of Jesus's birthday, he came to give you many good gifts.

Color the presents and ask Jesus to fill you up with his good gifts.

Pick which gifts from Jesus you would like to receive the most and **write the words in the gifts:** *Grace, Truth, Love, Kindness, Courage, Peace, Joy, Hope, Comfort*

29

Day 5: The Light Who Will Do Big Things through You

SCRITPURE

"But you, Bethlehem Ephrathah, are one of the smallest towns in Judah. But from you will come one who will rule Israel for me. He comes from very old times, from days long ago."

—Micah 5:2

The Old Testament prophet Micah prophesied (which just means God told him what would happen way before it *actually* did happen) that Jesus would be born in a town called Bethlehem. And then, it happened!

How many years before Jesus was born did the prophet Micah predict his birth? *Draw a box around your guess.*

700 years   100 years   450 years   2,000 years

If you drew a box around 700 years, you are correct!

Have you ever wanted to do something, but your parents or teachers told you that you couldn't yet because you were too young or little?

Draw a picture of which activity you would most like to do when you get older. Maybe it's a sport, a hobby, or a job.

DEVOTIONAL

It's hard to be told that we are too little or too young to do something we really want to do. The good news is that we don't have to *wait* to grow up to do important things for God! Remember in our verse for today that God chose a small town to host the birth of a very important event: the birth of Jesus!

Follow the clues below to spell out the name of the town Jesus was born in.

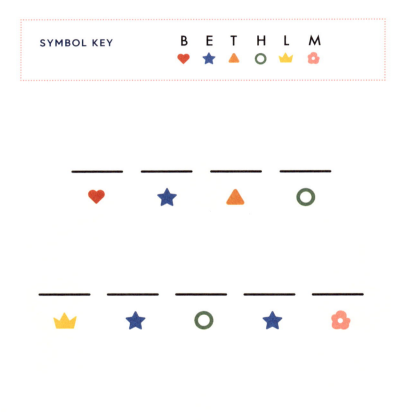

Let's pray together!

Jesus, I'm happy you were born in a small town. It may have been small, but you chose it to be home for your birth. Thank you that you have created me to do important things even when I'm young. Would you show me today what important thing you have for me to do?

In Jesus's name, amen.

GO

One way we can do important things for Jesus is to show his love and kindness to kids who don't have many friends. Can you think of one kid that you could show the love of Jesus to today?

Write their name here:

Now say a prayer for that person and try to show love to them in the next few days!

Day 6: The Light Who Brings You Peace

SCRIPTURE

A child will be born to us. God will give a son to us. He will be responsible for leading the people. His name will be Wonderful Counselor, Powerful God, Father Who Lives Forever, Prince of Peace.

—Isaiah 9:6

Have you ever been on a trip that felt like it was taking forever? Mary and Joseph traveled to Bethlehem on foot and by riding on a donkey. The trip was ninety miles long, and it probably took them a whole week to get there. It would have been a scary trip with predators like lions, bears, wild boars, and road bandits lurking by the road.

Check out this map of the route Mary and Joseph took from their hometown of Nazareth to Bethlehem.

> **Draw** a red circle around the city of Nazareth.
> **Color** the Dead Sea, Jordan River, and Sea of Galilee in blue.
> **Draw** a yellow star by Bethlehem.

DEVOTIONAL

How do you think Mary and Joseph felt making that long and difficult trip?

Can you think of a time when you had to do something difficult but also felt scared? While Mary and Joseph probably felt afraid about the trip (Mary was even about to have a baby), God protected them on their journey. He provided for them, and he will also protect and provide for you when you're faced with something scary.

Let's pray together!

Jesus, thank you for always being with us. One of your names is Prince of Peace. I ask for you to give me peace today when I feel scared or alone. Help me to remember to call upon you when I'm scared.

In Jesus's name, amen.

GO

Find a Post-it note or piece of paper. **Write "Jesus = Peace" on it.** Now, put it somewhere you will see it to remind you that you can ask Jesus to bring you peace anytime. Maybe on your mirror, on the wall of your room, your bedroom door, or your school binder.

Look at this example below and make your own on a extra piece of paper in your favorite color.

37

Day 7: The Light Who Provides

> **SCRIPTURE**
>
> She gave birth to her first son. There were no rooms left in the inn. So she wrapped the baby with cloths and laid him in a box where animals are fed.
>
> —Luke 2:7

DEVOTIONAL

When Mary and Joseph arrived in Bethlehem, there was no place for them to stay. Often, people will say that Mary and Joseph were put inside the innkeeper's barn. But did you know that back in those days, people had their animals stay in a portion of their home?!

The innkeeper had compassion for Mary and Joseph and let them stay in his own home where the animals were sheltered inside. The name Bethlehem means "house of bread." Isn't it cool that God chose a town whose name means "house of bread" to be the place where Jesus was born? Why is that cool, you ask? Well, bread provides strength and life for our physical bodies. Jesus came to provide life for us that never ends called eternal life.

Circle and find all the different types of bread, then color the picture.

KEY

Let's pray together!

Jesus, thank you for providing salvation for us! Thank you for also providing joy, peace, life, friendship, and wisdom to me. Jesus, today I need you to provide _____

Thank you for providing for me.

In Jesus's name, amen.

GO

Is there someone you know who needs something? Maybe it's a friend to invite to play on the playground, or maybe they need to be encouraged, or it could be an item that they need, like shoes. Ask Jesus if there is someone you can help meet a need for today.

Pray this prayer: "Jesus, show me if there is someone today I can help provide for, just as you have provided for me."

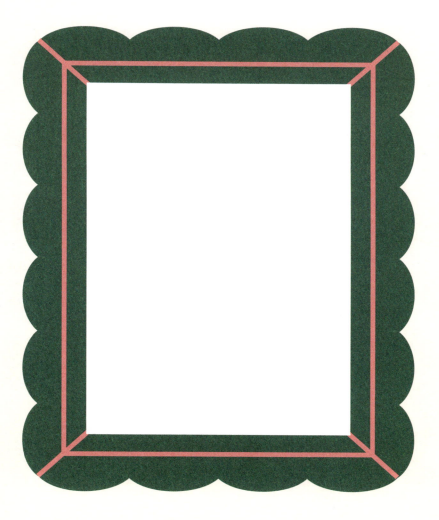

✏ **Write** down the names of the people you prayed for today and what you might do to provide for them this week!

Day 8: The Light Who Is a Good Shepherd

SCRIPTURE

That night, some shepherds were in the fields nearby watching their sheep. An angel of the Lord stood before them. . . . The angel said to them, "Don't be afraid, because I am bringing you some good news. It will be a joy to all the people. Today your Savior was born in David's town. He is Christ, the Lord."

—Luke 2:8a, 9–11

What's the dirtiest job you have ever done? Maybe it's scooping up your dog's poop, cleaning the toilet, or picking up stinky socks? We all have to do dirty jobs sometimes, but these jobs below are some of the dirtiest you can have.

Put an X through which job sounds the dirtiest to you.

Zoo cleaner

Rattlesnake catcher

Garbage pit technician

Sewer inspector

The shepherds had one of the dirtiest jobs during their time. They had to take care of and live with sheep who stunk and attracted bugs. They also had to defend their sheep from predators. It was a hard job, but they were committed to caring for and protecting their sheep.

God doesn't tell us in the Bible why he chose to tell the shepherds first that Jesus was born. One possible reason is because Jesus is called a Good Shepherd:

> "I am the good shepherd. The good shepherd gives his life for the sheep. . . . I know my sheep, and my sheep know me." John 10:11, 14b

Circle the sheep that label how Jesus is like a Good Shepherd to us.

Let's pray together!

Jesus, thank you for coming and being a Good Shepherd to us. Thank you for your care, comfort, and protection over me.

In Jesus's name, amen.

As Jesus the Good Shepherd cares for us, let's look for ways to care for the needs of others today. Ask Jesus this question: "Jesus, who can I show your care and comfort to today?" If you're not sure, look for ways to help people who are hurt today. It could be going to get a Band-Aid when your sister scrapes her knee, or offering to pray for a friend on the playground who's feeling sad.

Write any ideas you have in the sheep.

45

Day 9: The Light Who Is Worthy of Worship

SCRIPTURE

Suddenly a great company of the heavenly host appeared with the angel, praising God and saying, "Glory to God in the highest heaven, and on earth peace to those on whom his favor rests."

—Luke 2:13–14 (NIV)

DEVOTIONAL

The angels who appeared to the shepherds had a very important message to share.

Find all the words of their message in the word search below.

```
T E H G O G E A L H G H A V
A R T T O R G R E A T E R T
S T T D C D E A L E A R T H
R H T E G E E R L R Y L A P
R H I G H E S T F S O O E V
E E R I E E G G H R V C G O
I G E Y A P T C Y T A A T T
G G S V V L O I G E R E L R
Y A T E E E G E P V E A E V
T H F R N V F E H L V O E V
R F A E H F A R E G O H Y T
V S V R V O I G L O R Y A G
I L O G H O I A T G E A A P
C T R O E E L A T R P G O G
```

KEY:	glory	God	highest
heaven	earth	peace	favor

47

DEVOTIONAL

Have you ever had an important message to share? Usually, when we have something important or exciting to share, we blurt it out because we're so excited! The angels had the joy of announcing the birth of Jesus, and they started their message with praise. They said, "Glory to God in the highest heaven."

Do you have an exciting day or boring day ahead of you? Either way, it's so important to first focus our hearts and minds on God. One way to do that is through worship. We can worship with our words, like telling God how amazing he is, or with our actions, like doing something nice for someone. We can worship through song, or we can worship by writing a letter to God and telling him how thankful we are for him.

Let's pray together!

God, today, before I do anything else, I want to thank you for being a good and perfect Father. Thank you for sending Jesus to be born so I can be with you always. Thank you for being loving, kind, and good.

In Jesus's name, amen.

GO

List your favorite worship songs below. Now, turn on your favorite worship song and sing and dance along!

Day 10: The Light Who Is Good News

SCRIPTURE

Then the angels left the shepherds and went back to heaven. The shepherds said to each other, "Let us go to Bethlehem and see this thing that has happened. We will see this thing the Lord told us about." So the shepherds went quickly and found Mary and Joseph. And the shepherds saw the baby lying in a feeding box. Then they told what the angels had said about this child.

—Luke 2:15–17

Have you ever had really good news? Maybe you got 100 percent on your spelling test, school was canceled because of snow, or your parents said you were going to go to the park over the weekend.

Write or draw a picture on the blank postcard of some good news!

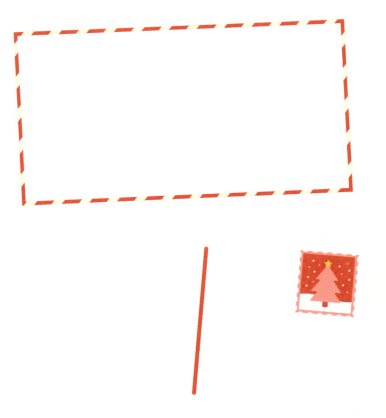

After the shepherds heard the good news that Jesus was born, the Bible says they went quickly to see him.

DEVOTIONAL

Color the sheep to help the shepherds get to where Jesus was born.

Not only did they go and worship Jesus, but they also told everyone around them the good news about Jesus. Is this the first time you've heard the good news that Jesus was born to save you from your sin? If so, Christmas is the perfect time to start a relationship with God! (If this is you, talk to your parents or a trusted adult about how to have a great relationship with God!)

Or maybe this is the one-hundredth time you're hearing the good news! If so, can you think about someone who may need to hear this good news?

Let's pray together!

Jesus, I praise you today for the good news that you were born! Thank you for coming to save me and everyone in the world from their sins so we could have a relationship with God! Thank you for your friendship, kindness, and love.

In Jesus's name, amen.

Think about someone who doesn't know the good news that Jesus was born. Tell them about Jesus! You can tell them while you play, write them a letter, or draw a picture to give them that shares this good news!

Day 11: The Light Who Came as a Servant King

SCRIPTURE

The angel said to her, "Don't be afraid, Mary, because God is pleased with you. Listen! You will become pregnant. You will give birth to a son, and you will name him Jesus. He will be great, and people will call him the Son of the Most High. The Lord God will give him the throne of King David, his ancestor. He will rule over the people of Jacob forever. His kingdom will never end."

—Luke 1:30–33

The shepherds weren't the only ones who received a special message through an angel. Nine months earlier, Mary was told that she would become pregnant with a boy and that she would name him Jesus. I'm sure Mary was very surprised to find out she'd be the mother of Jesus! The angel also told her who Jesus was going to be.

Follow the key and find a clue for who Jesus would be.

KEY:

1 - 🟡   2 - 🟢   3 - 🔴   4 - 🔵

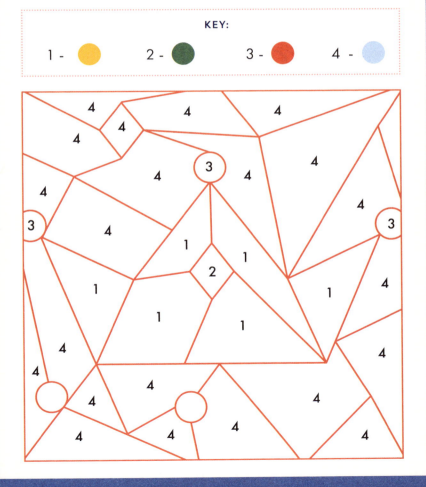

Jesus was a king! But he would be unlike any king the world had ever known. If you were king or queen for a day, what rules would you make? *Write a royal decree below with your rules.*

What were your rules? Were they rules about getting things that you wanted? Maybe you made a rule that you never had to do chores again and your brothers and sisters had to do all your chores, or maybe one of your rules was that your mom and dad had to give you all their money. A lot of kings and queens use their power to make themselves rich and to make themselves happy.

But Jesus did not come as this kind of king. He came to serve others, he was born to a poor family, and he served everyone around him, even washing the stinky feet of his own followers (called disciples)! Then he served every person by dying on the cross to save us from our sin and to give us eternal life.

Let's pray together!

Jesus, thank you for coming to us as a servant king. Thank you for showing us how to lead with love, service, and humility. Help me learn how to serve others as you did.

In Jesus's name, amen.

GO

Let's practice following Jesus's example by serving others. Jesus showed his heart to serve by washing the feet of his disciples (John 13:1–5). Today, I want you to wash the feet of at least one person in your family. As you wash their feet, tell them one reason why you are thankful for them.

Write in the feet the reasons you are thankful for your family so you can tell them while washing their feet.

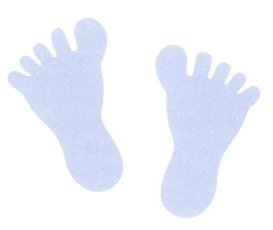

Day 12: The Light Who Gives You the Gift of Faith

SCRIPTURE

An angel of the Lord came and stood before Zechariah. When he saw the angel, Zechariah was confused and frightened. But the angel said to him, "Zechariah, don't be afraid. Your prayer has been heard by God. Your wife, Elizabeth, will give birth to a son. You will name him John. You will be very happy. Many people will be happy because of his birth. John will be a great man for the Lord. Even at the time John is born, he will be filled with the Holy Spirit. He will help many people of Israel return to the Lord their God."

—Luke 1:11–16 (excerpts)

Zechariah and Elizabeth were old and had never had a child. They prayed for a baby, and then one day an angel came and told Zechariah that his wife Elizabeth would have a baby named John. John would be Jesus's cousin and one day tell people about Jesus's coming.

Have you ever had a hard time believing that something good was true? Instead of being excited about the angel's message, Zechariah didn't believe the good news. Because he didn't believe, he lost one of his five senses until the baby was born.

Which of Zechariah's five senses stopped working when John was born? Circle your best guess!

Zechariah lost his ability to speak until after his son John was born and named. This story may feel kind of strange, but even if the Bible is hard to understand, we want to study it and ask God to help us understand what it's telling us today. One thing we know about this story is that God was promising something good to Zechariah. God is a good Father who gives good and perfect gifts. God is also a Father who speaks truth to us! When he tells us the truth, he wants us to trust and believe him even when it's hard. When we trust God's word even when it feels hard, it's called faith. Faith is a gift God gives us, and the amazing thing is, we can always ask God for more.

DEVOTIONAL

Below is a connect-the-dots picture. Sometimes being on a journey with God can feel a little bit like a connect-the-dots picture. We may kind of see what he is doing, but we need faith to give us courage to trust God to complete the picture.

Connect the dots below to reveal what we need.

Let's *pray* together!

Jesus, I ask that you give me the gift of faith today to trust that you are good and your promises are true.

In Jesus's name, amen.

GO — As you wrap Christmas presents, remember that faith is a gift God gives us when we ask.

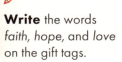

Write the words *faith, hope,* and *love* on the gift tags.

Day 13: The Light Who Is Trustworthy

SCRIPTURE

"You are blessed because you believed what the Lord said to you would really happen."

—Luke 1:45

The angel told Mary she was blessed because she believed God when she was told that she would be the mother of Jesus, even though that seemed impossible. One definition for the word *impossible* is "something that seems really hard," like keeping your room clean or maybe even learning math. Math was always a challenge for me as a kid! Whether you like math or not, these math facts are FUN!

The first fun math fact is about a prophecy. A prophecy tells something that is going to happen in the future. Guess how many prophecies were fulfilled by Jesus when he was born, lived, died, and was resurrected?

Circle your guess:

600   452   256   49

One of these prophecies was told by the prophet Micah in the Old Testament (more than four hundred years before Jesus was even born) when he said that Jesus would be born in Bethlehem (Micah 5:2).

A college professor once worked to see how likely it would be that someone could accurately predict 48 prophecies. He found that the chance of that happening is 10 ^ 157. That little ^ means you have to add 157 zeros to 10.

That number would look like this:

1000,000,000,000,000,000,000,000,000,000,000,000,000,000,000,000,000,000,000,000,000,000,000,000,000,000,000,000,000,000,000,000,000,000,000,000,000,000,000,000,000,000,000,000,000,000,000,000,000,000,000,000,000,000,000,000,000,000,000

That's very, very unlikely!

(Answer: 452 prophecies were fulfilled by Jesus!)

DEVOTIONAL

So now imagine the chances of all 452 prophecies coming true—that would be even more zeroes! We can trust God because he has proven himself trustworthy. Everything that was prophesied surrounding Jesus's life *really did* happen!

If you're struggling to trust that Jesus is who he says he is, ask him to give you the gift of faith. Faith is a gift that helps us trust God even when we don't fully understand the plan.

Let's pray together!

God, I ask to have the gift of faith like Mary had. When you speak through your word or to my heart, please give me faith to believe you are who you say you are and that you will do what you say you will do!

In Jesus's name, amen.

GO

I made some Christmas cookies for you! But instead of the normal stars, snowmen, and Christmas trees, I made them into the number 452 to help us remember how many prophecies Jesus fulfilled!

Color the cookies below.

65

Day 14: The Light Who Gives You Family

SCRIPTURE

When Elizabeth heard Mary's greeting, the unborn baby inside Elizabeth jumped. Then Elizabeth was filled with the Holy Spirit. She cried out in a loud voice, "God has blessed you more than any other woman. And God has blessed the baby which you will give birth to."

—Luke 1:41–42

DEVOTIONAL

Have you ever had exciting news that you couldn't wait to share? When you have exciting news, who do you want to tell first?

Write their name here: _____

Mary went to visit her cousin, Elizabeth, to share about Jesus growing inside her. Both Elizabeth and Mary had babies whose births were foretold by angels (Luke 1:5–25; Luke 1:26–38). Their babies would also have a special relationship with each other. Elizabeth's baby, John the Baptist, would preach about Jesus and baptize him. Even though Mary and Elizabeth were excited about their babies, they may have been nervous about the unknowns too.

When we're excited, nervous, or sad, God gives us friends and family to encourage us. And when we follow Jesus, we don't just get our family—we also have access to brothers and sisters in Christ who are all following and trusting in Jesus. This is called the family of God.

Do you like baking and decorating gingerbread men and women at Christmastime? *Color in the words in icing that show how brothers and sisters in Christ can help each other.*

67

Let's pray together!

Thank you, God, for giving me your family to encourage, serve, pray, and share life with. Help me to look for ways to love and serve my brothers and sisters in Christ.

In Jesus's name, amen.

GO

Think about a brother or sister in Christ, write down their name, and circle a way that you can encourage them today!

Name

Serve **Pray** **Share**

✏️ **Draw or write down** how you will do what you circled.

Day 15: The Light Who Is Worthy of Your Time

SCRIPTURE

After Jesus was born, some wise men from the east came to Jerusalem. They asked, "Where is the baby who was born to be the king of the Jews? We saw his star in the east. We came to worship him."

—Matthew 2:1b–2

The wise men traveled a long way to worship Jesus. We do not know their exact journey, but it probably took four to five months to reach Jesus. It also would have been a hard journey through the desert on camels. I've never ridden on a camel before, but I can imagine it would be bumpy and that there would have been no air conditioning, movies, or audiobooks to listen to, either.

Check out this map that shows the journey the wise men probably took. Use a <u>green</u> marker and *put a green check mark* at the wise men's starting point. Find a <u>red</u> marker and *trace the journey* the wise men took. Now use a <u>yellow</u> marker to *put a star* at their destination, Nazareth.

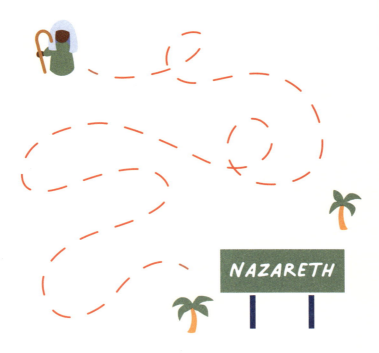

DEVOTIONAL

Jesus is worthy of our worship for so many reasons. Check out these musical notes below and *color in which things about Jesus make you want to worship him the most.*

He heals

He died for my sins

He loves to talk to me

He comforts me

He guides me

He loves me

72

Let's pray together!

Jesus, thank you for the example of the wise men who traded their comfort to come and worship you. Help me to be willing to give up my things and time to worship you.

In Jesus's name, amen.

GO

The wise men gave up their time and comforts to worship Jesus. We may know we need to spend time worshipping Jesus and reading our Bible, but it can be hard to actually make the time in our busy lives.

Write down or draw pictures on the clock below of all the things that take up your time every day. You may want to include school, chores, and other activities.

Now look again at the list you made in the clock. Put a check mark next to some things you could take some time from so you can have more time to worship Jesus.

Here are some ideas: Maybe instead of reading a comic book before bed, you can read your Bible or listen to a worship song. Maybe give up some screen time or video game time to worship God by serving a sibling or taking time to pray. If you're not sure, ask your mom or dad to help you come up with some other ideas.

Write down your ideas in the blanks.

Day 16: The Light Who Speaks to You

SCRIPTURE

The wise men heard the king and then left. They saw the same star they had seen in the east. It went before them until it stopped above the place where the child was. When the wise men saw the star, they were filled with joy.

—Matthew 2:9–10

When Jesus was born, God gave the wise men an unusual sign. What was the sign they received? Hint: Look in the scripture above and circle the sign!

The wise men had studied the skies, stars, and planets for many years, so they could tell that the North Star was leading them to go and meet a king. The Bible is full of examples of people who heard from God in crazy ways. To find out what some of those ways were, cross out any time you see the word *go* to reveal the message!

Here's an example: *Thisgo pugozzle wigoll be fungo!* (Answer: This puzzle will be fun!)

Ggood loves to talgok to us. The Bibgole tells us somego times when God talkgoed to people in cragozy ways.

God talked to Bagolaam through his dongokey, Moses heagord from God through a burngoing bush, and Kingog Belshazzar was warngoed by God by reading writgoing on a wagoll.

While God may not speak to you through an animal, a bush, or writing on a wall, the great news is that Jesus does want to speak to you! There are different ways we can hear Jesus speak to us. Often, it's through a quiet voice inside our hearts, through reading the Bible, while we are singing a worship song, or when a friend shares something called a testimony. A testimony is a story of how Jesus has changed someone's life.

Let's pray together!

Jesus, thank you for speaking to me in so many ways. Help me learn to hear from you and always be watching for you to be speaking and showing me the way to go.

In Jesus's name, amen.

GO

We find out what God is like by reading the Bible. Today, let's practice hearing from God through reading his word, the Bible. The Bible is like a letter God sent to us, to let us know what he is like, what he thinks about us, how we should live, and give us hope for the future.

Think like a detective and look for clues of what God may be speaking to you through this Bible verse:

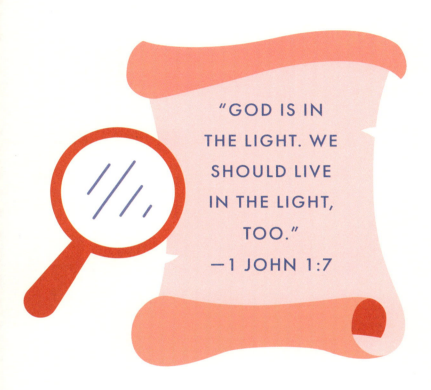

"GOD IS IN THE LIGHT. WE SHOULD LIVE IN THE LIGHT, TOO."
—1 JOHN 1:7

Answer these questions:
1. What does this verse say about God?

2. What does this verse say about you?

Day 17: The Light Who Delights in You

SCRIPTURE

They saw the same star they had seen in the east. It went before them until it stopped above the place where the child was. When the wise men saw the star, they were filled with joy.

—Matthew 2:9b–10

Recognize the verse for the day? We're reading the same scripture again but talking about a different part today! God spoke to the wise men through a star. One of the reasons he may have done this is because that's what the wise men loved. They had devoted their life to studying the stars, moon, planet, and skies. Today, that job is called an astronomer.

I used to think that I could only learn about God or experience him if I was sitting down studying the Bible or sitting in church, but that's not true. It's important to study the Bible and go to church, but God loves to speak to us even in the middle of our everyday life. He loves to speak to us while we're doing things we love to do. He may speak to you while you're playing soccer; you may feel his love and delight while you twirl on point in ballet; you may learn something about God's creativity while you're listening to a song or experience his beauty while on a nature walk.

The wise men loved to study the sky. God has made you to experience joy while you are doing certain things. It's his plan and delight that you learn about him while you do your favorite things.

DEVOTIONAL

Draw a picture of you doing your favorite thing inside the snow globe.

82

Let's pray together!

God, thank you for creating me to love

_____

(fill in your favorite things to do)

Please show me how to experience you and learn more about you while I'm doing those things.

In Jesus's name, amen.

GO — Look up at your snow globe and remember what your favorite thing is to do. Today, find some time to do your favorite thing (you can do it now if you have time)! While you're doing your favorite activity, ask God this question: God, will you help me learn about you today while I do my favorite thing?

After you do your favorite thing, come back and **draw a picture or write down** anything you learned about God while you were doing your favorite activity.

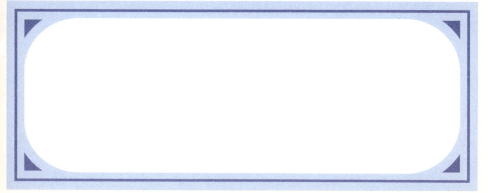

Day 18: The Light Who Is Worthy of Your Best Gifts

SCRIPTURE

They went to the house where the child was and saw him with his mother, Mary. They bowed down and worshiped the child. They opened the gifts they brought for him. They gave him treasures of gold, frankincense, and myrrh.

—Matthew 2:11

The wise men were important men in their country. They may have been kings or men with a lot of money and power. The gifts they brought Jesus were expensive and showed the great honor they were placing upon him. Each gift had a special meaning and pointed to who Jesus is:

- Gold represents royalty. Jesus is our king.

- Frankincense is a symbol of holiness, as it was usually burned in the temple as an offering to God. Jesus is holy.

- Myrrh was an oil that was used in someone's death and burial. Jesus would live a perfect life, die on the cross, and defeat death for us! Jesus died for our sins.

Complete the crossword puzzle on the next page and remember that just like the wise men brought their best gifts to Jesus, we can bring our hearts, time, and gifts to Jesus because we love him and know how special he is.

Across

2. A gift brought to Jesus from the wise men. This gift is an oil that was used in someone's death and burial.

5. Three of these followed a star all the way from their house to see baby Jesus and bring him gifts!

6. A gift brought to Jesus from the wise men. This gift represents royalty.

7. This is what happens when someone passes away. *(Hint: For Jesus, this happened in a cave.)*

9. A gift brought to Jesus from the wise men. This gift is a symbol of holiness and was burned in the temple as an offering to God.

Down

1. "For you are a holy people to the Lord your God; the Lord your God has chosen you to be a people for Himself, a special _____ above all the peoples on the face of the earth." —Deuteronomy 7:6 (NIV)

3. The leader of a royal family. *(Hint: He gets to wear a crown!)*

4. This word means "to be set apart" and it's often used to describe Jesus! Jesus taught us lots of ways to become like this.

5. This is something we do at church on Sunday morning! *(Hint: It's the part where we sing!)*

8. We give these to each other at Christmas as a way to celebrate Jesus!

KEY:

Gold	Gift	Myrrh	Wise men	Treasure
King	Holy	Burial	Worship	Frankincense

Let's pray together!

Jesus, I want to bring the best that I have to you today. Help me to give to you just like the wise men did. Thank you for being our king, thank you for your holiness, and thank you for dying for me.

In Jesus's name, amen.

Turn back to Day 3 and look at the snowflake. Take note of the unique abilities God has given you. Take a moment to ask God this question: *God, out of all the unique talents you've given me, which one should I give to you?*

The wise men wouldn't have wrapped presents in paper and with bows like we do now. Their gifts would have been brought in containers that looked something like below.

 Write in the containers which gift God has given you that he wants you to use to worship him.

Day 19: The Light Who Leads You

SCRIPTURE

A child will be born to us. God will give a son to us. He will be responsible for leading the people.

—Isaiah 9:6a

This verse tells us that Jesus will be our leader. One sign of a good leader is that they understand, listen to, and know the people they are leading. Practice being a good leader by finding out which Christmas treats your family or friends would pick from this plate. *Write their name beside each treat you think they would choose.*

DEVOTIONAL

Jesus took time to get to know all types of people. Whether it was a tax collector like Zacchaeus, a religious leader like Nicodemus, or little children, Jesus loved and served the people around him, showing us that he is a leader worthy to be followed. Jesus also left us a perfect example to follow as we love those around us. Even people who are different than we are! Jesus knows everything about you, and he wants to lead. When we follow Jesus, we're able to make the best choices and live the life he calls us to.

Let's pray together!

Jesus, I want you to lead my life. I love that you know everything about me and know what is best for me. Help me learn how to hear you better, follow you every day, and love those around me like you have loved me!

In Jesus's name, amen.

GO

One way to lead like Jesus is to spend time with people and learn about them. Jesus spent time with fishermen on their boats, children playing, and families eating. Jesus laughed, cried, and enjoyed his friends and family.

Spend time with someone in your family today by doing this fun Christmas Mad Lib together. Ask your family member to fill in the blanks with names, verbs, nouns, and more. Then read it aloud together!

Name of a friend: _____

Adjective: _____

Noun: _____

Noun: _____

Noun: _____

Family member's name: _____

Adjective: _____

Animal: _____

Food: _____

Your name: _____

Dear _____ [Name of friend],

I am so _____ [Adjective] it is Christmas! I love celebrating the birth of Jesus by decorating the _____ [Noun], singing _____ [Noun], and hanging up _____ [Noun]. This year, I am really excited because _____ [Family member's name] said they would dress up like a snowman! I know Christmas is about Jesus, but I can't help but feel _____ [Adjective] about getting gifts. The gift of Jesus is the best present we could ever receive, but I am also hoping I get a _____ [Animal] and that we eat _____ [Type of food] on Christmas Day!

Love,

_____ [Your name]

93

Day 20: The Light Who Is Your Wonderful Counselor

SCRIPTURE

His name will be Wonderful Counselor, Powerful God, Father Who Lives Forever, Prince of Peace.

—Isaiah 9:6b

DEVOTIONAL

How many names do you have? Most people usually only have three names—a first, middle, and last name. Guess what? Jesus has 198 names and titles given to him in the Bible! For the next few days, we're going to talk about four of the names the prophet Isaiah gave to Jesus.

In the verse on page 94, circle *Wonderful Counselor* and write it on the Christmas ornament below.

Wonderful means "inspiring delight; extremely good; or marvelous." Or another way to put it would be "full of wonder"! It's easy to feel wonder at Christmastime when we see all the beautiful decorations and experience fun parties and gifts. But a relationship with Jesus can fill us with wonder every day, even during hard times.

The second part of Jesus's name is Counselor. People receive counsel or may visit a counselor when they need to know what to do or when they're feeling sad or have a hard problem to solve. Another word could be Helper.

DEVOTIONAL

Jesus is our extremely good Helper!

The Christmas trees we usually put up in our homes are called evergreens. The name *evergreen* means always, you guessed it, green! God has made our hearts to be like an *evergreen* tree, always alive and growing because Jesus is inside of us and will help us with any hard thing we go through.

Look at the Christmas tree ornaments—they have faces that show different things you may be feeling today or this week.

Circle the faces that show how you have been feeling this week.

Let's pray together!

Thank you, Jesus, for being the Wonderful Counselor. I ask that you would help me be full of wonder today at the amazing Savior and friend you are. I'm so grateful that you're always with me, through the good and the hard!

In Jesus's name, amen.

 GO Jesus is a counselor who wants to bring us comfort when we're sad, listen when we're excited, and give us peace when we're feeling scared. Anytime we have a problem, we can go to Jesus and ask for his help. He is a safe place for us to come to.

As you look at the faces of different feelings you have, I want you to imagine bringing all those feelings to Jesus. You can say this: "Jesus, I give you all my feelings. Thank you for being with me. I give you any hard feelings today and ask for your peace to fill me up."

 After giving your feelings to Jesus, **draw** a picture of your face. How did it make you feel?

Day 21: The Light Who Is Full of Power

SCRIPTURE

Jesus did many other miracles before his followers that are not written in this book. But these are written so that you can believe that Jesus is the Christ, the Son of God. Then, by believing, you can have life through his name.

—John 20:30–31

Forty-two of the miracles Jesus did during his three years of ministry on earth are written about in the Bible. We know from reading our verse today that there were many more miracles Jesus did that were not written down in the Bible. Remember our verse from last week listing some of the names of Jesus?

> His name will be Wonderful Counselor, Powerful God, Father Who Lives Forever, Prince of Peace. —Isaiah 9:6b

One of the names of Jesus is "Powerful God." Underline that twice in the verse above!

When Jesus walked the earth, the way he proved that his power was from God was through performing miracles. Here are a few miracles Jesus did. *Circle the miracle you would have wanted to see the most!*

- Jesus feeds five thousand people with three loaves of bread and two fish (Matthew 14:13–21).
- Jesus provides tax money through coins in a fish's mouth (Matthew 17:24–27).
- Jesus raises Lazarus to life from the dead (John 11:38–44).
- Jesus heals two blind men (Matthew 9:27–31).
- Jesus walks on water (Matthew 14:22–33).

Did you know that Jesus is still doing miracles today? When you accept Jesus as the Lord and Savior of your life, he sends his Holy Spirit to live in you. How is that for a miracle?! That means his power is inside of you. And Jesus wants to do miracles through you, even today! The best way to see Jesus do a miracle is to pray for someone when you see a need, like a sick person, a friend who is sad, or a person who's in trouble. Ask Jesus to do a miracle by healing them, comforting them, or giving them peace. And when Jesus answers that prayer, be sure to thank him for that miracle!

Let's pray **together!**

Jesus, thank you for being a powerful God. Help me to remember to pray for miracles when I need help or see a friend in need.

(If you can think of a person who needs a miracle, like a sick friend who needs to be healed or a sad family member who needs Jesus's joy or salvation, you can pray for that now.)

Pray this: Jesus, I ask for a miracle for _____. Would you give them [what they need: healing, joy, salvation, peace, money]?

In Jesus's name, amen.

GO

Let's play charades!

Cut a sheet of paper into five pieces. Write one of Jesus's miracles on each piece of paper. Feel free to add more miracles if you want!

Jesus feeds five thousand people with three loaves of bread and two fish.

Jesus provides tax money through coins in a fish's mouth.

Jesus raises Lazarus to life from the dead.

Jesus heals two blind men.

Jesus walks on water.

Now, gather your friends or family together for the game! Put all the pieces of paper in a hat or bowl. Now, one person draws a clue from the hat and acts it out (with no words) while the others guess! Whoever guesses correctly gets to act out the next miracle!

Day 22: The Light Who Is the Way

SCRIPTURE

Jesus answered, "I am the way. And I am the truth and the life. The only way to the Father is through me. If you really knew me, then you would know my Father, too. But now you do know him, and you have seen him."

—John 14:6–7

Jesus is a part of something called the trinity. The trinity has three parts: the Father (God), the Son (Jesus), and the Holy Spirit. Remember our verse from last week listing some of the names of Jesus?

> His name will be Wonderful Counselor, Powerful God, Father Who Lives Forever, Prince of Peace. —Isaiah 9:6b

One of Jesus's names is the "Father Who Lives Forever" because Jesus is God's son and they are one because of the trinity. Underline that name twice in the verse above!

DEVOTIONAL

Another way to understand the trinity is to think about an egg. An egg has three parts: the shell, egg white, and yolk. Each of these parts is different and has a unique purpose and identity, but they are all a part of the egg.

Jesus's life on earth and his death on the cross paved the way for us to have a relationship with our Father God, who lives forever! Look at our scripture on the previous page and answer this question:

The only way to the Father is through _____.

(Answer: Jesus)

Let's pray together!

Jesus, thank you for being the way, the truth, and the life! Thank you for making a way for me to have a relationship with my perfect Father God. Help me to understand and experience the trinity more today.

In Jesus's name, amen.

GO

Listen to the song "For unto Us a Child Is Born" by Handel. As you listen, color in the poinsettia. Plants help us understand the trinity a little more because they have many parts: stems, flowers, leaves, and the roots underneath. Each of the parts has an important role in the plant, and together they make one plant!

Color the poinsettia and **write** the words *Father*, *Son* and *Holy Spirit* on the different leaves.

105

Day 23: The Light Who Is the Prince of Peace

SCRIPTURE

His name will be Wonderful Counselor, Powerful God, Father Who Lives Forever, Prince of Peace.

—Isaiah 9:6b

DEVOTIONAL

For four whole days, we've been studying the names of Jesus in Isaiah 9. Today, we will explore one more of his names: Prince of Peace. Jesus brings peace into the craziest and most difficult times.

To explain, let's look at a story from Mark 4:35–41. One day, Jesus and his disciples were aboard a boat when a big storm came upon them. When the storm came rolling in with thunder and lightning, Jesus was taking a nap and didn't even wake up. He just kept sleeping, but his disciples were all awake.

In the thought bubbles, write what you think the disciples were thinking about the storm and about Jesus sleeping through it!

When Jesus finally woke up, he told the disciples not to worry because he had authority (that means he was the boss) over the storm. He then spoke to the storm and said, "Peace be still." The storms obeyed, and it became calm. As you can imagine, the disciples were very happy that the storm was over and were amazed that Jesus brought peace to the storm.

Did you know it's the same in our life? Jesus can bring peace to any situation we face. He is the Prince of Peace. If something is crazy, hard, or scary, we can ask Jesus to bring his peace and calm.

Let's pray together!

Before we begin, is there someone in your life you think needs some extra peace today? Maybe it's you or a friend or family member. Pray this prayer over yourself or someone else.

Jesus, thank you for being the Prince of Peace. Please bring your peace to _____. Jesus, help me to remember that you are the source of peace because you are the Prince of Peace.

In Jesus's name, amen.

GO

Play a game of hot (peace) and cold (scared) with your family or friends. As you play this game, remember that the one thing that will always bring you peace is Jesus. When we have Jesus inside of our hearts, we have access to peace at all times.

HOW TO PLAY

Take the baby Jesus from your nativity scene (make sure you ask your parents if you can borrow it) or draw a picture of baby Jesus and use that.

Now, hide baby Jesus somewhere and tell the players to start looking for him. When the players are getting closer to where baby Jesus is hiding, make the peace sign by holding up your index and pointer finger; when they are getting farther away, make a scared face.

Day 24: The Light Whose Kingdom Will Grow

SCRIPTURE

Power and peace will be in his kingdom.
It will continue to grow.

—Isaiah 9:7a

Where is the king's kingdom? *Circle the picture you think is correct.*

That was a trick question!

Whichever picture you circled is correct! Why? Because wherever the king goes, he carries the kingdom with him. When Jesus is our king, wherever Jesus is, *that* is where his kingdom is. Look at the verse for today and underline what two things it says will be in Jesus's kingdom.

When Jesus is in your heart, you carry the king and his kingdom wherever you go: school, the basketball court, the park, your friend's house, or the grocery store. Jesus's kingdom isn't confined by a wall or a small group of people. Anywhere Jesus's followers go, that's where his kingdom goes. That means you can bring Jesus's kingdom of power and peace anywhere.

Let's pray together!

Jesus, thank you that your kingdom goes with me wherever I go. Help me release your power and peace wherever I go today and every day.

In Jesus's name, amen.

GO Think about how you can bring the power and peace of Jesus's kingdom to a neighbor, friend, or family member today. Here are some ideas that your whole family can participate in.

Caroling: Get your family together, put on festive Christmas outfits, and go caroling around your neighborhood. Be sure to include a song about the hope and peace Jesus brings, like "Joy to the World" or "O Come Let Us Adore Him." Write down your song list so you're prepared:

Give a card: When you go to a store or restaurant over the next few days, ask your parents if you can encourage the cashier or server. People working around Christmastime are usually tired and wishing they were with their family. Take time to thank them for checking you out or serving you, ask if you can pray for them, or bring along a homemade thank-you card! If you make a card, add some encouragement from Scripture such as:

> For to us a son is given . . . and he will be called Wonderful Counselor, Mighty God, Everlasting Father, Prince of Peace.
> —Isaiah 9:6–7

Day 25: The Light Who Gives Eternal Life

SCRIPTURE

"I am the light of the world. The person who follows me will never live in darkness. He will have the light that gives life."

—John 8:12b

DEVOTIONAL

Merry Christmas! Today is the day we celebrate the light of the world, Jesus, being born. It's such a special day! What fun traditions will your family do today?

As you open presents, eat yummy food, and spend time with family and friends, I want you to remember that Jesus is the light that came to this world for you! Jesus was born, lived a perfect life, died on the cross, and was raised from the dead, defeating death and sin for you! He wants to save you from your sin so you can be with God forever in heaven and so you can spend every day with him inside of you. He wants to fill you up with his love, peace, and joy every day.

Gather your family (make sure you have an adult around), grab a few candles, turn off the lights, and then, with an adult's help, light the candles one by one. *Then take a moment to think about these questions and share your answers together!*

What was it like in the room before the candles were lit?

What was it like in the room after the candles were lit?

DEVOTIONAL

What was the difference between when one candle was lit versus all the candles being lit?

What happens when we try walking in a dark room?

What happens when we try walking in a room that is full of light?

When Jesus was born, it changed *everything!* He came to save every person who was lost because of their sin. Just like lighting candles makes the room bright for us to see where we're going, Jesus brings light into our hearts so we can see and experience him. With Jesus as our Lord and Savior, we will know the way to go.

Jesus also brings light into our hearts so we can bring hope and light into the lives of people who are hurting. Just like the lit candles brought light into the room, wherever we go, we bring the light of Jesus with us and it fills the world with love, joy, peace, and hope.

Let's pray together!

If you haven't made a decision to make Jesus the Lord and Savior of your life, today is the perfect day to decide to follow Jesus. You can pray this prayer (and don't forget to share your decision with your parents, grandparents, or another trusted adult):

Jesus, thank you for coming as the light of the world. I ask that you come into my heart and save me from my sins. I want you to be the Lord and Savior of my life, and I want to follow you every day. Fill me up now with your Holy Spirit.

In Jesus's name, amen.

If you have already prayed a prayer like the one above, pray this:

Jesus, thank you for being the light of the world. Thank you for being my Lord and Savior as I celebrate Christmas today. Help me to remember this day is about honoring you and help me to shine your light every day!

In Jesus's name, amen.

GO

Ask your family or friends to help you host an **"Eyewitness News Report" show.** You can be the news reporter and ask family and friends to be the following characters: Mary, Joseph, Angel, Shepherd, Wise Man, Innkeeper, and Donkey.

Ask them questions for your news show about what it was like to meet Baby Jesus. You can use these questions and then write in some of your own.

Write down the answers to your interview questions.

If your family and friends aren't sure what to say, you can teach them all the things you have learned in this Advent devotional about the many people who saw Jesus around the time he was born.

What is your name? ☐

What is your job? ☐

How did you feel when you heard that Jesus was born?

☐

EYEWITNESS #2

What is your name?

What is your job?

How did you feel when you heard that Jesus was born?

EYEWITNESS #3

What is your name?

What is your job?

How did you feel when you heard that Jesus was born?

"Power and peace will be in his kingdom. It will continue to grow."

—Isaiah 9:7a

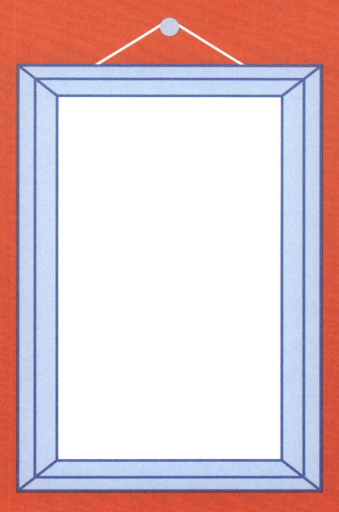

Draw a picture of yourself with your completed journal.

About
First15

Spending consistent time alone with God can be a struggle. We're busier—and more stressed—than ever. But still, we know it's important to spend unhindered time with our Creator. We know we need to read his word, pray, and worship him.

First 15 bridges the gap between desire and reality, helping you establish the rhythm of meaningful, daily experiences in God's presence. First 15 answers the critical questions:

- Why should I spend time alone with God?
- How do I spend time alone with God?
- How do I get the most out of my time alone with God?
- How can I become more consistent in my time alone with God?

And by answering these questions through daily devotionals, we help people practice the rhythm of meeting with God while experiencing the incredible gift of his loving presence.

To learn more about First 15, download our app or visit our website: *First15.org*. The First 15 devotional is also available via email and podcast.